T is for Texas

Anne Bustard

VOYAGEUR PRESS

Printed in Hong Kong.

89 90 91 92 93 5 4 3 2 1

Library of Congress Cataloging-in-Publication Data

Bustard, Anne, 1951-
    T is for Texas : text / by Anne Bustard.
        p.   cm.
    Summary: Photographs and text introduce the letters of the alphabet and the sights and symbols of Texas.
    ISBN 0-89658-113-6 : $12.95
    1. Texas—Juvenile literature. 2. Alphabet—Juvenile literature.
[1. Texas. 2. Alphabet.]   I. Title.
F386.3.B86   1989
976.4—dc20
[E]
                                                                                89-35633
                                                                                   CIP
                                                                                    AC

Published by Voyageur Press, Inc.
P.O. Box 338
123 North Second Street
Stillwater, MN 55082
Toll-free 800-888-9653
In Minn 612-430-2210

Voyageur Press books are also available at discounts in bulk quantities for premium or sales-promotion use. For details contact the Marketing Manager. Please write or call for our free catalog of publications.

To Ray, Cindy, Pansy and Elliott

To Maggie
With ♡ as BIG as
TEXAS!

Anne Bustard
1990

Anne Bustard currently lives in Austin, Texas, and is co-owner of a very successful book-store for children.

Aa

**is for armadillo,
suited with armor.**

Bb

is for boots,
crafted by hand.

Cc

**is for cowboy,
with tools of his trade.**

Dd

**is for dinosaur track,
a sign of the past.**

Ee

**is for enchiladas,
served hot on a plate.**

Ff

is for flag,
symbol of the Lone Star State.

Gg

is for Gulf Coast,
a good place for fun.

Hh

is for "howdy,"
a Texas "hello."

Ii

is for Indian Paintbrush, a wildflower in bloom.

Jj

is for jalapeño,
a hot juicy pepper.

Kk

**is for kick-off,
the start of a game.**

...standing proudly on the range.

Mm is for mockingbird, state bird of Texas.

Nn

is for NASA,
exploration
in space.

pumped from the ground.

Pp is for pecans, tucked in their shells.

Qq

is for quilt,
stitched with
great care.

Rr is for rodeo.
Ride, cowboy, ride!

Tt
is for Texas,
the friendly state.

Uu

**is for university,
on graduation day.**

Vv

is for "The Valley," where vegetables grow.

Ww

is for whooping cranes, kept safe from extinction.

Xx

s for XIT,
an old ranch brand.

Yy

is for "y'all,"
heard everywhere in Texas.

Zz

is for zillions
and zillions of
bluebonnets,
matching the
Texas sky.

Photo credits:

Texas Parks and Wildlife Department: *A*
Texas Highway Department: *B,C,F,L,O,P,Q,R,V,W,X,Z*
NASA: *N*
George O. Miller: *D,E,G,H,I,J,K,M,S,T,Y, Title page*
Jay Godwin: *U*

Front cover photos by Texas Highway Department and Texas Parks and Wildlife Department